RECORD-BREAKING HUMANS

Jon Richards and Ed Simkins

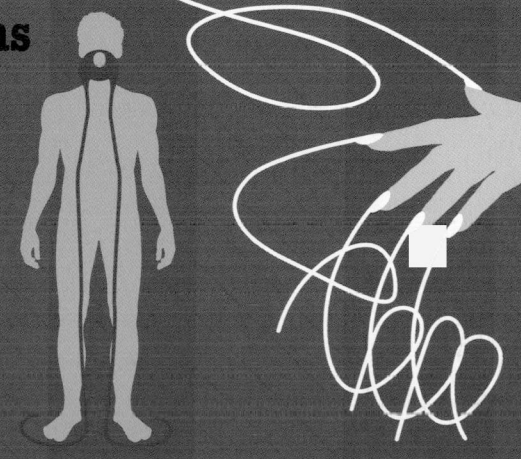

WAYLAND

CONTENTS

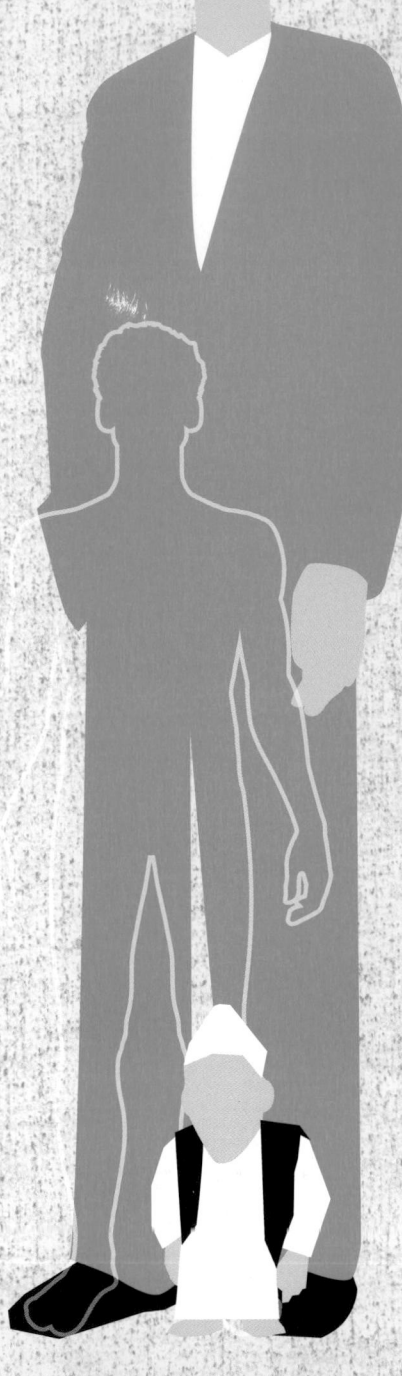

pages 8–9
Meet the tallest and shortest people and compare your hand to the biggest in the world.

WELCOME!

From the tallest to the shortest, the fastest to the strongest, and the oldest to the richest, this book looks at amazing human record-breakers. It uses stunning icons, graphics and visualisations to show you how human beings keep pushing their potential to the absolute limits.

pages 16–17
See just how far some divers can swim underwater on a single breath of air.

pages 18–19
Compare the size of the largest film cast with the population of Iceland.

pages 28–29
Measure the world's largest book next to a giraffe.

SUPER CELLS

<----------------------------->

The trillions of cells in your body come in all shapes and sizes. The largest are just visible to the naked eye, while the longest stretch the whole length of your legs. Together, these amazing cells create tissues that form the building blocks of your body.

The largest human cell is the egg or ovum. One of these can measure about 1 mm across.

The smallest cell is the sperm, which measures about **0.06 mm** long – about 10 could fit on the full stop at the end of this sentence.

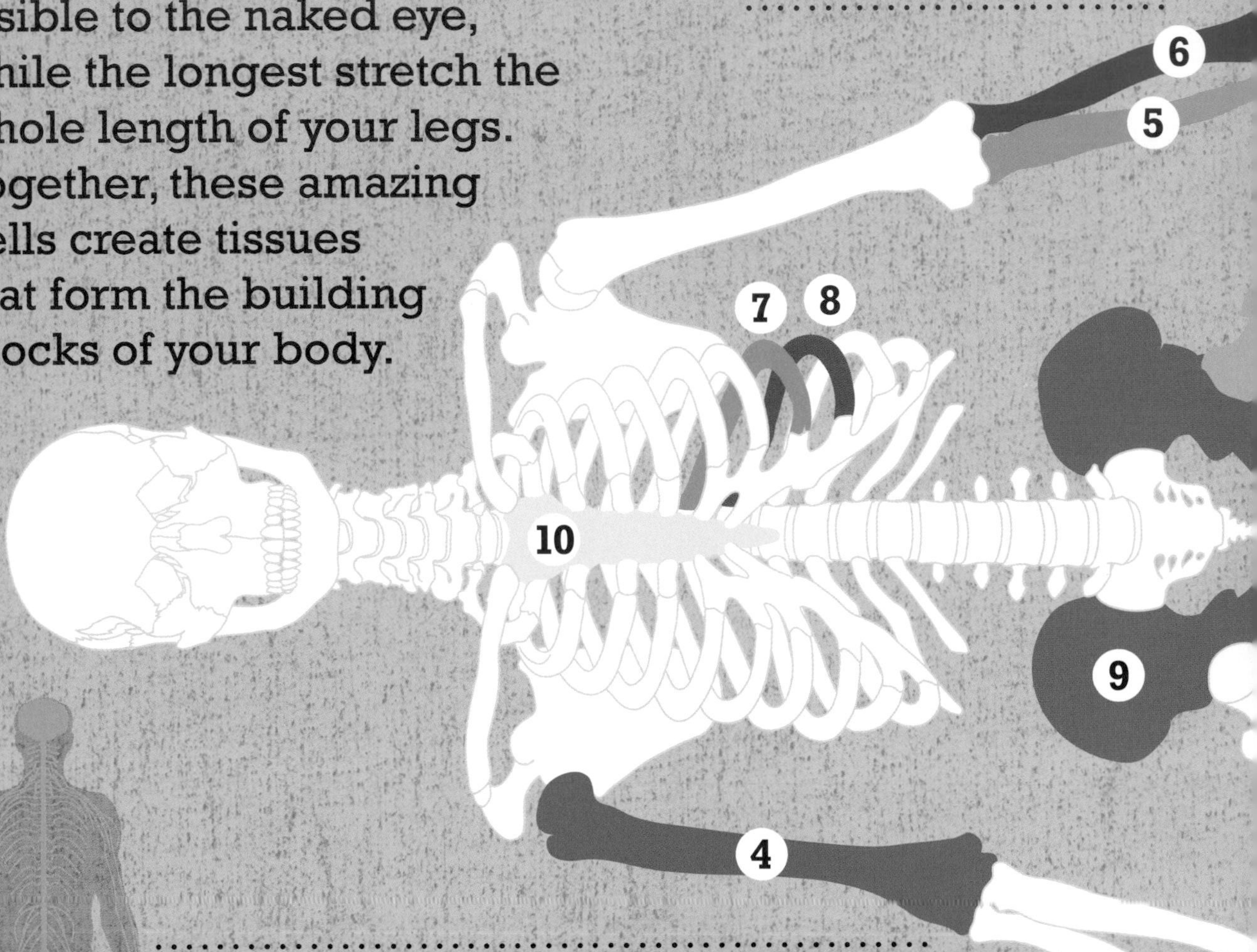

6

5

7 **8**

10

9

4

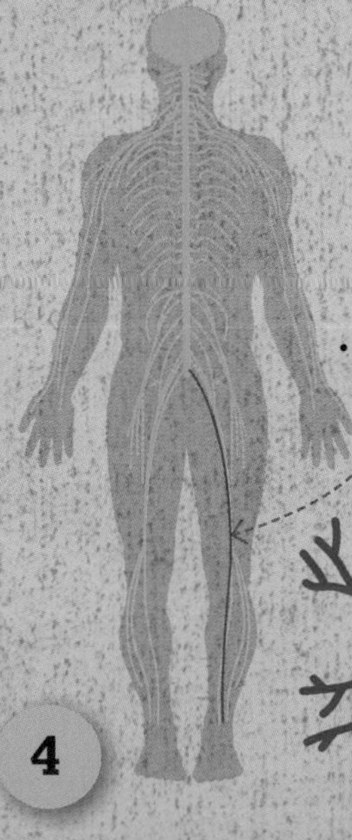

Motor neurone

The **longest cells** in the human body are motor neurones that stretch from the base of the **spine** to muscles in the **toes**.

Longest cell

They can be up to 1 m long.

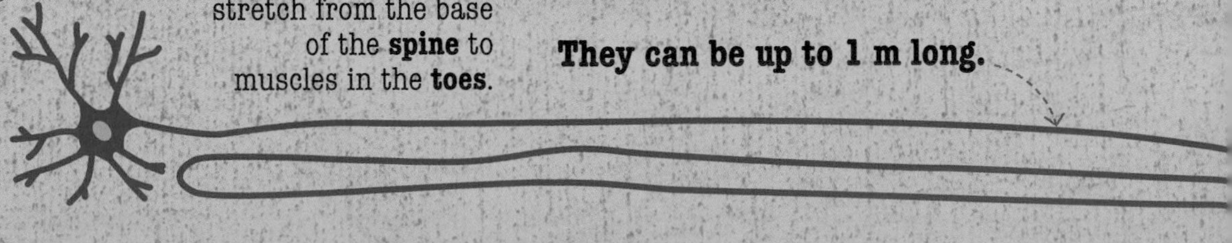

Magnified x 70

Egg

Sperm

LONGEST BONES IN THE HUMAN BODY
(AVERAGE LENGTH – CM)

1. **Femur (thigh bone) – 50.5**
2. **Tibia (shin bone) – 42.9**
3. **Fibula (lower leg) – 40.4**
4. **Humerus (upper arm) – 36.6**
5. **Ulna (inner lower arm) – 28.2**
6. **Radius (outer lower arm) – 26.4**
7. **Seventh rib – 24.4**
8. **Eighth rib – 23.1**
9. **Innominate bone (hip bone) – 18.5**
10. **Sternum (breast bone) – 17.0**

1

2

3

Long leg

The leg of an adult human is just under **1 m** long.

In comparison, a giraffe's leg is nearly twice as long, about **1.8 m** in length.

40%
Skeletal muscle makes up about 40 per cent of your body's mass.

In an adult weighing 70 kg, that means **28 kg** is muscle, which is more than the weight of **two gold bars.**

Muscle tissue

ORGANS AND SYSTEMS

<--------------------------------->

The largest, heaviest organ in your body covers you completely, protecting you from the outside world. Your other organs perform an amazing range of tasks, allowing you to live, grow and survive.

Brain bits

The cerebrum is the upper portion of the brain and is its largest part, making up about...

... 85% of the brain's mass.

The brain is the fattest organ in the human body.

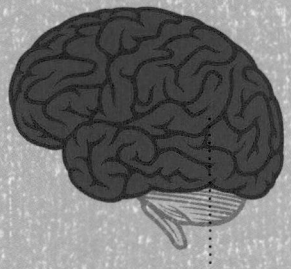

About 60% of the brain is fat.

9 Thyroid

This butterfly-shaped organ is found in your neck and produces several chemicals that tell your body how to behave.

35 g

4 Lungs

These large sacs fill with air when you breathe in so that oxygen passes into your body and carbon dioxide passes out.

1,090 g

3 Brain

Protected by your skull, this organ receives signals from all over your body, and weighs as much as two basketballs.

1,263 g

5 Heart

This muscular organ is part of the blood, or circulatory, system. It weighs a little less than a tin of soup.

315 g

Skin is usually 1–2 mm thick. The thinnest parts of your skin are your eyelids (about 0.5 mm thick), while parts of the upper back have skin that is 5 mm thick.

1–2 mm

0.5 mm

5 mm

Your body has about **5.6 litres of blood**, equivalent to 5.6 litre bottles of water. This blood is pushed by the heart through the body **three times every minute.**

In one day, the blood travels a total of **19,000 km** – that is four times the distance across the **US**, from coast to coast.

4

Blood system facts

7

Spleen
This organ acts as a blood reserve. It also removes old red blood cells and helps the immune system.

170 g

8

Pancreas
This organ produces chemicals which tell your body how to act, as well enzymes, which break down food.

98 g

Your stomach is a stretchy bag of muscle that gets bigger and smaller as food enters and leaves it. An adult stomach can expand to hold up to 1.5 litres of food.

1

Skin
This organ covers your entire body and prevents water loss. It weighs about as much as four bricks.

10,886 g

6

Kidneys
These two organs lie on either side of your back. They filter your blood, removing harmful waste products.

290 g

2

Liver
Part of your digestive system, this organ helps you to break down and process what you eat.

1,560 g

10

Prostate
This small, walnut-size male organ makes seminal fluid, which sperm cells travel in.

20 g

BODY EXTREMES

Growing the longest body parts can take decades of dedicated care and attention. Other body part records, however, come a little more naturally.

1 Longest hair

Xie Qiuping of China has been growing her hair for more than 40 years. It is now nearly three times as long as a bed.

5.627 m

2 Longest nails

Lee Redmond of the USA spent nearly 30 years growing and looking after her nails.

8.65 m (total length)

3 Longest nose

When measured from the bridge of the nose to its tip, Mehmet Ozyurek of Turkey has the longest nose of any living person.

8.8 cm

Life size!

4 Longest moustache

Ram Singh Chauhan of India grew a moustache that was longer than a Volkswagen Beetle.

4.29 m

196 cm

132 cm

5 Longest legs

Svetlana Pankratova from Russia holds the record for the world's longest legs. They make up more than two-thirds of her total height!

132 cm

Most fingers and toes

Akshat Saxena from India was born with a condition called polydactylism – he had more fingers and toes than normal.

14 fingers (7 on each hand)
20 toes (10 on each foot)

6

7 Largest hands

Robert Wadlow of the USA had hands that measured 32.3 cm from the wrist to the tip of the middle finger.

32.3 cm

8 Largest feet

He also had the largest feet ever measured. They were 47 cm long!

US size 37AA or UK size 36

1.8-m-tall man

Robert Waldow's shoe size

Average men's shoe size (US size 10 or UK size 9)

9 Tallest person

In fact, Robert Wadlow holds the record as the tallest person who has ever lived.

2.72 m

10 Shortest person

In contrast, Chandra Bahadur Dangi from Nepal is the shortest living person and is only one-fifth of Wadlow's height.

54.6 cm

Life size!

LIVING LONG

With improvements in medicine and diet, it is now not uncommon for someone in a rich country to live 100 years or more. However, there are still many poor countries where people have low life expectancy.

Growing old

By 2050, studies predict that there will be **1.56 billion** people over the age of **65**, making up about **17 per cent** of the world's population.

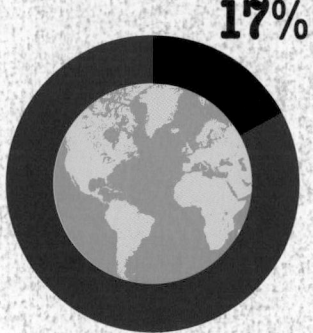

17%

1.56 billion

Aging Americans

By 2050, the number of people over 65 in the USA will **more than double**. It is predicted that the number of people aged **over 100** will soar from 72,000 to 834,000.

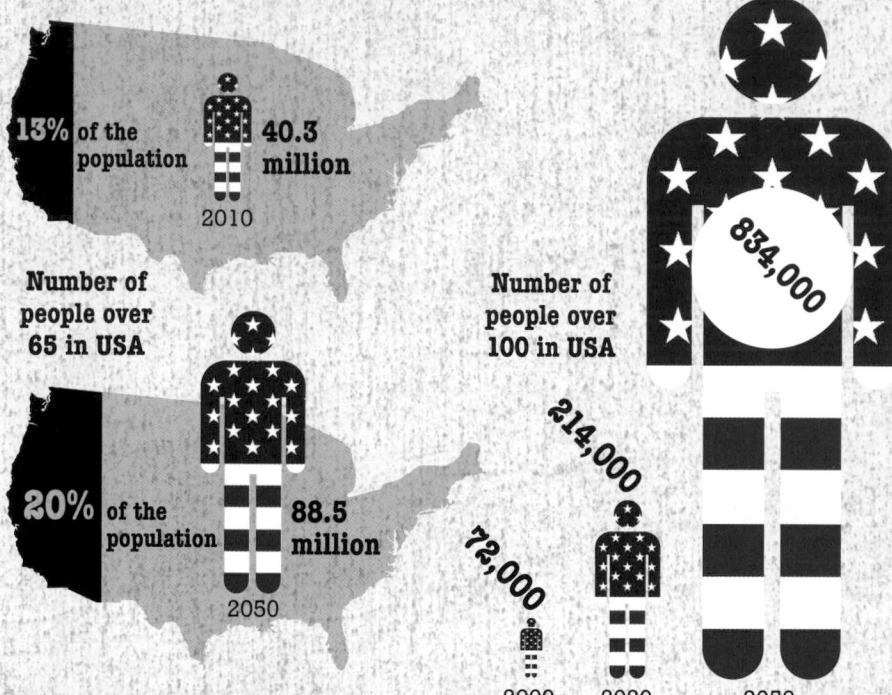

13% of the population — **40.3 million** — 2010

Number of people over 65 in USA

20% of the population — **88.5 million** — 2050

Number of people over 100 in USA

72,000 — 2000
214,000 — 2020
834,000 — 2050

Oldest person who's ever lived

Jeanne Louise Calment from France lived for 122 years 164 days, from 21 February 1875 to 4 August 1997.

Born 21 February 1875

1876: Alexander Graham Bell invents the telephone.

1903: The Wright Brothers make the first powered flight at Kitty Hawk, North Carolina, USA.

1928: The first transatlantic television signal is sent between London and New York.

1875   1885   1895   1905   1915   1925

Lowest life expectancy

PLACES WHERE PEOPLE LIVE THE LONGEST
(LIFE EXPECTANCY – YEARS)

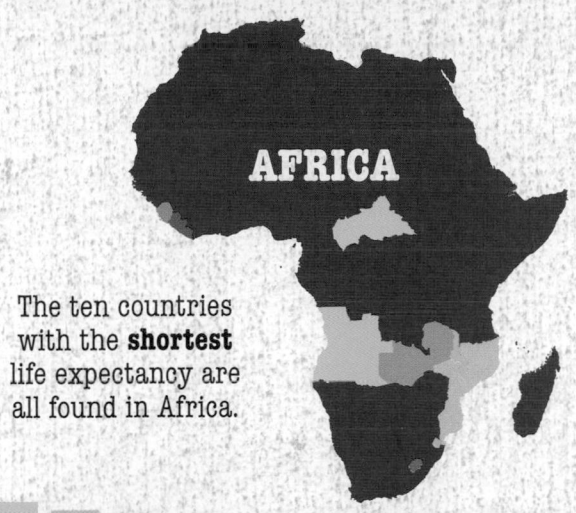

AFRICA

The ten countries with the **shortest** life expectancy are all found in Africa.

1. **Switzerland – 82.70**
2. Japan – 82.59
3. **Iceland – 82.36**
4. Spain – 82.33
5. **Italy – 82.09**
6. Australia – 81.85
7. **Sweden – 81.80**
8. Israel – 81.76
9 **France – 81.67**
10. Norway – 81.30

- Central African Republic – 44.5 years
- Malawi – 43.8 years
- Djibouti – 43.4 years
- Liberia – 41.8 years
- Sierra Leone – 41.2 years
- Mozambique – 41.2 years
- Lesotho – 40.4 years
- Zambia – 38.6 years
- Angola – 38.2 years
- Swaziland – 31.9 years

A Swiss man born in 1900 had a life expectancy of **51**. One born in 2000 can expect to live to **85**. By 2050, some studies show that **2.2 million** Swiss, nearly **30 per cent**, will be older than 65.

1900   2000

Aging Swiss

1010
0101

1938: The world's first freely programmable computer, the Z1, is built by Konrad Zuse.

1961: Yuri Gagarin becomes the first person to orbit Earth.

1969: Apollo 11 mission lands the first people on the Moon.

1978: Louise Brown, the world's first test tube baby, is born.

Dies 4 August 1997

1945   1955   1965   1975   1985   1995

ON THE RUN

The world's fastest sprinters can run at 45 km/h, but they can only manage this pace for a short time. Other runners need more endurance than speed to take part in races that cross deserts or climb skyscrapers.

In just **four years**, two Jamaican sprinters managed the set **five** new world 100-m records.

100-m record progression

16 August 2009

16 August 2008

31 May 2008

9 September 2007

14 June 2005

9.5   9.6   9.7   9.8   9.9   10

| 9.58 seconds | 9.69 seconds | 9.72 seconds | 9.74 seconds | 9.77 seconds |

← — — — — — — Usain Bolt — — — — — — — → ← — — — Asafa Powell — — — →

How far in 10 seconds?

These bars show the distance a sprinter, a marathon runner, a record-breaking swimmer and a person moving at normal walking pace could cover in 10 seconds.

Olympic sprinter – 100 m

Marathon runner – 57.15 m

Olympic swimmer – 24 m

Walking pace – 16 m

← — — — — — — — — — — **10 seconds** — — — — — — — — — — →

RUNNING RECORDS

1. **100 metres: Usain Bolt (Jamaica) – 9.58 secs**

2. 110 metre hurdles: Aries Merritt (USA) – 12.8 secs

3. **200 metres: Usain Bolt (Jamaica) – 19.19 secs**

4. 400 metres: Michael Johnson (USA) – 43.18 secs

5. **800 metres: David Lekuta Rudisha (Kenya) – 1 min 40.91 secs**

6. 1,500 metres: Hicham El Guerrouj (Morocco) – 3 mins 26 secs

7. **5,000 metres: Kenenisa Bekele (Ethiopia) – 12 mins 37.35 secs**

8. 10,000 metres: Kenenisa Bekele (Ethiopia) – 26 mins 17.53 secs

9. **Half marathon: Zersenay Radese (Eritrea) – 58 mins 23 secs**

10. Marathon: Dennis Kimetto (Kenya) – 2 hours 2 mins 57 secs

Ultra Marathon

Ultra-marathon runner Marshall Ulrich ran **4,930 km** from San Francisco to New York in just **52 days**. That is nearly **95 km** every day!

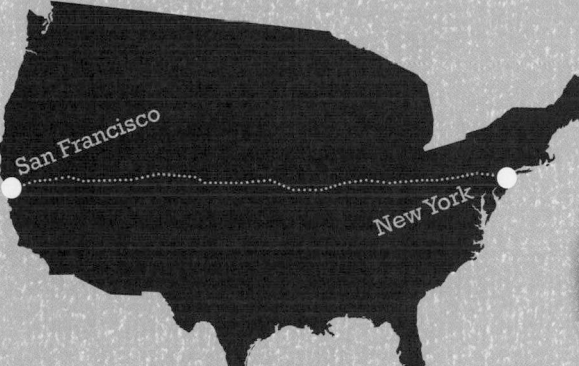

San Francisco

New York

At the 1896
Olympic Games in Athens, Spiridon Louis of Greece won the gold medal in the marathon, completing the race in a time of 2 hours, 58 minutes, 50 seconds.

MARATHON DE SABLES

Competitors in the Marathon des Sables have to run 251 km (that's the same as running 9.5 marathons!) across the north African desert in six days, experiencing temperatures over 50°C.

Empire State

Every year, more than **400 athletes** race up the Empire State Building in New York City. They have to run up to the **86th floor**, climbing **1,576 steps** on the way. The winner usually completes the race in a little over **10 minutes**.

86th floor

320 m

THROWING AND JUMPING

Power, speed and agility are vital to smash throwing and jumping records. Throwers will try to go farther than anyone before, while jumpers will go for distance and height to become world record holders.

Standing jumps

The **standing** high jump and long jump appeared at the Olympic games until 1912. Athletes tried to jump as **high** or as **long** as they could from a standing start. Today, competitors take a **run-up** before jumping.

Record distance – 3.71 m

Standing long jump

Record height – 1.48 m

Standing high jump

Throwing records

GRAPE THROW AND CATCH
A J Henderson managed to throw a **grape**, run and catch it in his mouth over a distance of 21.18 m, which is about the length of two buses.

LIGHT BULB
A **light bulb** was thrown for a record 32.53 m by Bipin Larkin.

10 m

0 m

THROWING AND JUMPING RECORDS

1. **Javelin:** Jan Zelezny (Czech Republic) 25 May 1996 – 98.48 m

2. **Discus:** Jürgen Schult (East Germany) 6 June 1986 – 74.08 m

3. **Hammer:** Yuriy Sedykh (USSR) 30 August 1986 – 86.74 m

4. **Shot put:** Randy Barnes (USA) 20 May 1990 – 23.12 m

5. **Long jump:** Mike Powell (USA) 30 August 1991 – 8.95 m

6. **Pole vault:** Renaud Lavillenie (France) 15 February 2014 – 6.16 m

7. **Triple jump:** Jonathan Edwards (UK) 7 August 1995 – 18.29 m

8. **Standing high jump:** Jonas Huusom (Denmark) 27 August 2011 – 1.48 m

9. **High jump:** Javier Sotomayor (Cuba) 27 July 1993 – 2.45 m

10. **Standing long jump:** Arne Tvervaag (Norway) 11 November 1968 – 3.71 m

High jump styles

Over the years, athletes have used and developed different high jump styles. Today's jumpers use the **Fosbury flop**, developed by Dick Fosbury in 1965.

scissors

straddle

western roll

Fosbury flop

LONGEST PEANUT THROW
Former world champion hurdler Colin Jackson holds the record for the longest **peanut** throw, at 37.92 m.

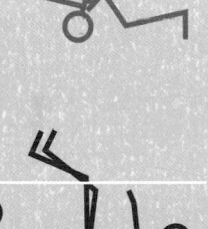

EGG THROW AND CATCH
This record is held by Willie O'Donevan and Warren McElhone, and stands at 71.2 m.

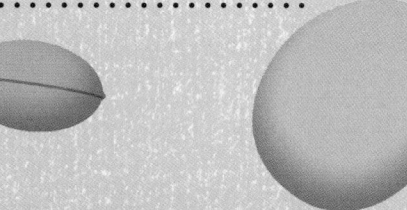

SWIMMING AND DIVING

Some deep divers use a line and a weighted sled to carry them down.

Take a deep breath and plunge beneath the surface with these amazing water sport records. These can involve diving from a great height, plunging to the ocean's depths or racing through a swimming pool.

Free diving

← 100 m →

← 281 m →

Dynamic apnea with fins involves swimming as far as possible **underwater** on one breath. The record is held by Goran Colak from Croatia, and it is **281 m** – that's nearly three football pitches.

Deepest dive

Herbert Nitsch of Austria dived to a depth of **214 m** and returned to the surface on a single breath! That's more than twice the height of the **Statue of Liberty**.

214 m

93 m

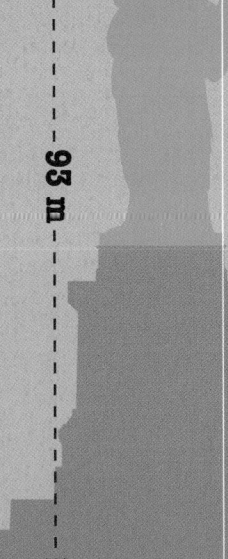

Diving

Cliff divers jump off a platform that's 27 m above the water – as tall as a nine storey building.

27 m

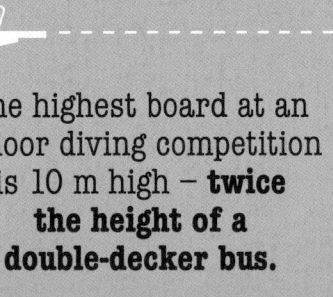

The highest board at an indoor diving competition is 10 m high – **twice the height of a double-decker bus.**

SWIMMING RECORDS

1. **50 m freestyle: Cesar Cielo (Brazil) – 20.91 secs**

2. **50 m breaststroke: Cameron vd Burgh (South Africa) – 26.67 secs**

3. **50 m backstroke: Liam Tancock (UK) – 24.04 secs**

4. **50 m butterfly: Rafael Munoz (Spain) – 22.43 secs**

5. **100 m freestyle: Cesar Cielo (Brazil) – 46.91 secs**

6. **100 m breaststroke: Cameron vd Burgh (South Africa) – 58.46 secs**

7. **100 m backstroke: Aaron Peirsol (USA) – 51.94 secs**

8. **100 m butterfly: Michael Phelps (USA) – 49.82 secs**

9. **4 x 100 m freestyle: USA – 3 mins 8.24 secs**

10. **4 x 100 m medley: USA – 3 mins 27.28 secs**

Longest unassisted swim

Chloe McCardel of Australia swam for **42 hours** and covered **142 km** – more than **four times** the distance across the English Channel.

142 km
in 42 hours

England

English Channel

France

Swimming strokes

There are four types of **stroke** used at swimming competitions; freestyle (or front crawl), backstroke, breaststroke and butterfly. **Medleys** are a special type of race where swimmers use all four styles, one after the other.

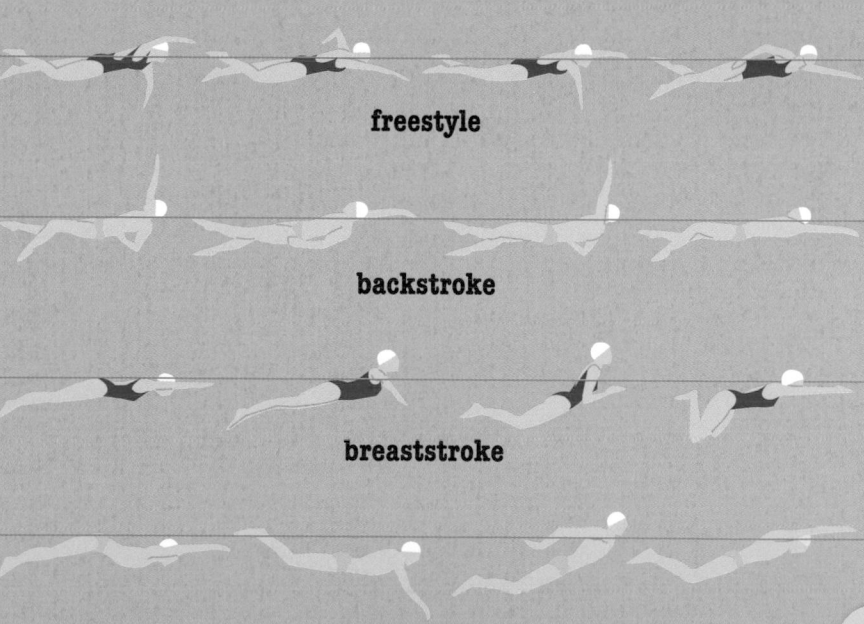

freestyle

backstroke

breaststroke

butterfly

SUPER STRONG

<-->

These people are the strongest on the planet! They can lift, pull and carry enormous weights, many times their own body weight, and regularly take part in competitions to see who is the strongest.

Weightlifting techniques

Breaking **power lifting** and **weightlifting** records involves trying to lift as much as possible using the techniques shown here.

Snatch

Clean and jerk

Deadlift

Squat

Bench press

Lance Karabel of the USA holds the record for the squat, carrying 455 kg – that's almost the same as the weight of an adult male grizzly bear.

Dariusz Slowik from Poland threw a **48-kg** washing machine a distance of **3.5 m** to set a new record.

POWER & WEIGHTLIFTING RECORDS

1. **Snatch (men):** Behdad Salimkordasiabi (Iran) – 214 kg

2. **Clean and jerk (men):** Hossein Rezazadeh (Iran) – 263 kg

3. **Combined (snatch and clean and jerk) (men):** Hossein Rezazadeh (Iran) – 472 kg

4. **Snatch (women):** Tatiana Kashirina (Russia) – 151 kg

5. **Clean and jerk (women):** Tatiana Kashirina (Russia) – 190 kg

6. **Combined snatch and clean and jerk (women):** Tatiana Kashirina (Russia) – 334 kg

7. **Squat:** Lance Karabel (USA) – 455 kg

8. **Bench press:** Alan Baria (USA) – 387.5 kg

9. **Dead lift:** Vugar Namazov (Azerbaijan) – 370 kg

10. **Combined squat, bench press, dead lift:** Lance Karabel (USA) – 1,095 kg

World's strongest

Mariusz Pudzianowski of Poland has won the World's Strongest Man competition five times. Aneta Florczyk, also of Poland, holds the women's record with four wins. Here are some of the events that competitors take part in.

Farmer's Walk

Overhead log lift

Atlas stones

Vehicle pull

Reverend Kevin Fast from Canada lifted **22 people** who were standing on a platform.

Manjit Singh

Manjit Singh of the UK pulled a double-decker London bus weighing **8 tonnes** (about the same as 1.5 elephants) **21.2 m** using ribbons tied to his hair.

He holds more than **30 strength records**, including pulling a bus with **54 people** on board with one hand.

He also pulled a **Vulcan jet bomber** weighing in at **92 tonnes** (the same as 18.5 elephants) a distance of **15 cm** using a harness.

THE SILVER SCREEN

Lights, camera, action! Since the first movies were made at the end of the 19th century, people have been producing films that continue to set records for money taken, number of people appearing, size and endurance!

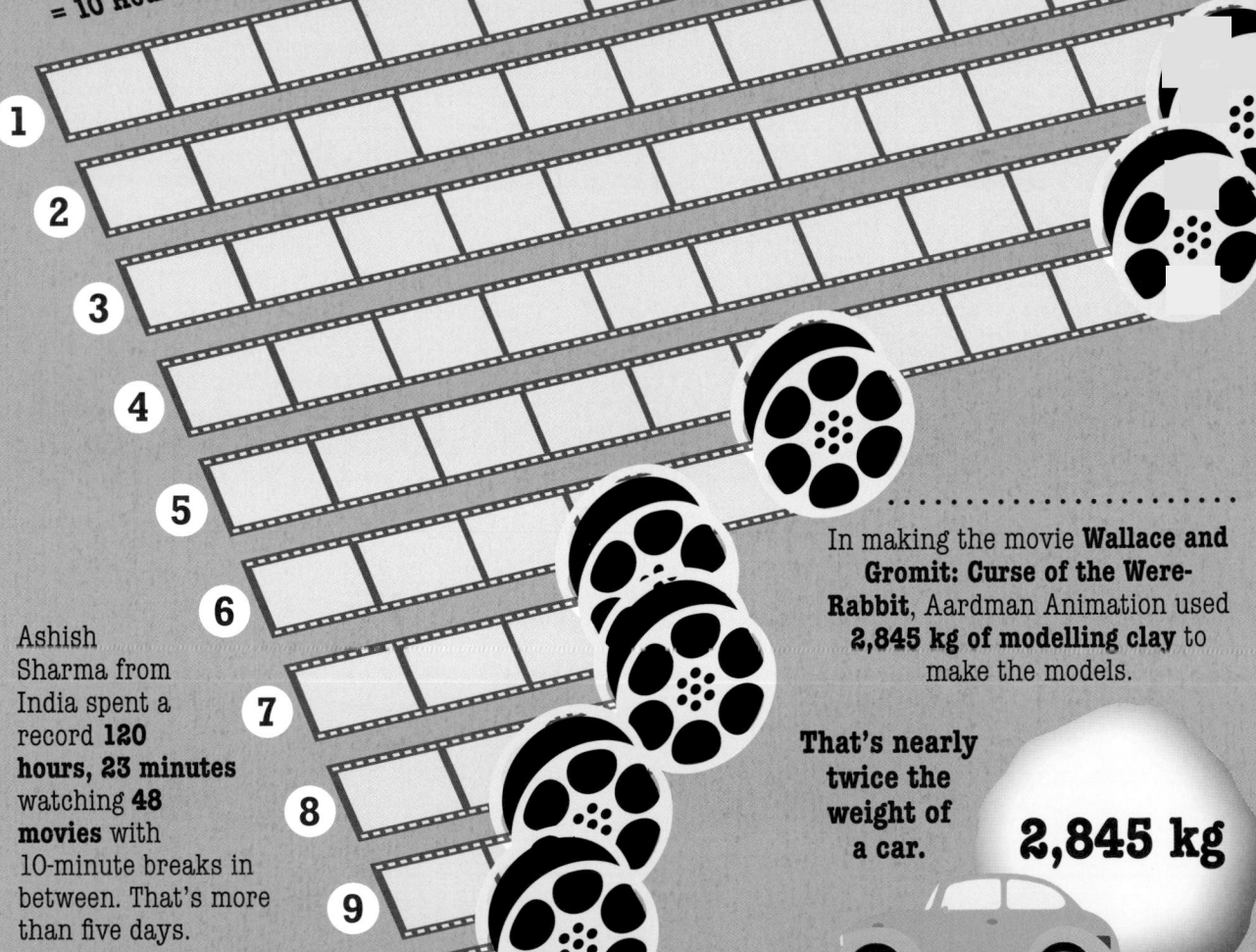

= 10 Hours

1
2
3
4
5
6
7
8
9
10

Ashish Sharma from India spent a record **120 hours, 23 minutes** watching **48 movies** with 10-minute breaks in between. That's more than five days.

In making the movie **Wallace and Gromit: Curse of the Were-Rabbit**, Aardman Animation used **2,845 kg of modelling clay** to make the models.

That's nearly twice the weight of a car.

2,845 kg

Highest-grossing film

When adjusted for inflation, the highest-grossing movie of all time is **Gone with the Wind**. Its adjusted figure comes in at **US$5,362,000,000**. In contrast, Avatar (2009), which holds the record for the highest-grossing movie (unadjusted) took **US$2.8 billion**.

GONE WITH THE WIND

CLARK GABLE
VIVIEN LEIGH
LESLIE HOWARD OLIVIA DE HAVILLAND

Tiniest film

Measuring just **45 by 25 nanometres** a 60-second stop-motion film made by IBM is the smallest movie ever made. It was made using individual molecules, placing and moving them for each shot. The film tells the story of a boy playing with a ball.

Largest cast

More than **300,000 actors and extras** appeared in one scene for the movie **Gandhi** (1982), that is nearly the same size as the entire population of Iceland.

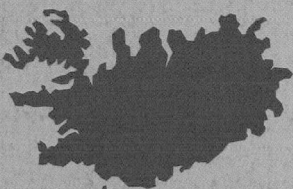

LONGEST FILMS EVER MADE

1. **Modern Times Forever (2011) – 14,400 minutes (240 hours OR 10 days)**

2. **Cinématon (1984) – 11,220 minutes (187 hours OR 7 days, 19 hours)**

3. **Beijing 2003 (2004) – 9,000 minutes (150 hours OR 6 days, 6 hours)**

4. **Matrjoschka (2006) – 5,700 minutes (95 hours OR 3 days 23 hours)**

5. **The Cure for Insomnia (1987) – 5,220 minutes (87 hours OR 3 days, 15 hours)**

6. **The Longest Most Meaningless Movie in the World (1970) – 2,880 minutes (48 hours)**

7. ****** (1967) – 1,500 minutes (25 hours)**

8. **The Clock (2010) – 1,440 minutes (24 hours)**

9. **A Journal of Crude Oil (2008) – 840 minutes (14 hours)**

10. **Tie Xi Qu: West of the Tracks (2003) – 551 minutes (9 hours, 11 minutes)**

THAT'S RICH!

These people are the richest on the planet. They have accumulated huge amounts of wealth in industries such as computer software, airlines, telecommunications and investments.

Where do the billionaires live?

This map shows the **distribution** of the world's billionaires, with most living in **Europe and Russia** and the fewest found in **Australasia**.

Total number of billionaires **1,682**

North America **441**

26%

6%

Latin America **94**

RICHEST PEOPLE

1. **Bill Gates (USA) – US$78.9 bn**
2. **Carlos Slim Helu (Mexico) – US$78.8 bn**
3. **Warren Buffett (USA) – US$66.1 bn**
4. **Amancio Ortega (Spain) – US$55.1 bn**
5. **Larry Ellison (USA) – US$47.1 bn**
=6. **Charles Koch (USA) – US$39.7 bn**
=6. **David Koch (USA) – US$39.7 bn**
8. **Christy Walton (USA) – US$36.9 bn**
9. **Jim Walton (USA) – US$35.5 bn**
10. **Liliane Bettencourt (France) – US$34.1 bn**

Bill Gates, the world's richest person, has given away more than US$30 billion to charitable causes since 2000, through the Bill and Melinda Gates Foundation.

The city with the most billionaires is Moscow. It has...

... 84 billionaires with a combined wealth of US$366 bn.

This is enough wealth to purchase nearly **750,000 gold bullion bars**

It is also more than the Gross Domestic Product (annual earnings) of the country of South Africa.

Europe and Russia
505 **30%**

Moscow

29%

Asia
488

1.5%

Africa
25

Middle East
108

6.5%

Australasia
21

1%

Where can money take you?

The total combined wealth of the world's billionaires comes to **US$6.4 trillion.**

Enough to give everyone on the planet more than **US$900.**

Changed into quarters (25-cent coins), this money would create a stack of coins **44.8 million km tall**. That's long enough to stretch nearly **1,120 times around the globe** or more than...

... 58 times to the Moon and back.

WORKS OF ART

These paintings were created by some of the best-known artists who ever lived. Although not all achieved success in their lifetimes, their works have gone on to sell for hundreds of millions of dollars.

1894–1895

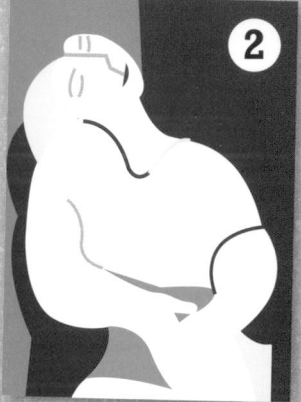

1932

Least valuable art collection

The Museum of Bad Art in Boston, USA, holds the record for the least valuable art collection. Its 573 works are worth just US$1,197.35, **or US$2.09 each.**

1969

1948

Vincent Van Gogh produced more than **2,000** works of art, but he only sold **one** while he was alive.

1953

1907

Oldest art

Made by Neanderthals around **40,000 years ago**, scratches found on a cave wall in Gibraltar may be Europe's oldest art.

MOST EXPENSIVE WORKS OF ART

1. **The Card Players, Paul Cezanne – US$259 million**
2. La Rêve, Pablo Picasso – US$155 million
3. **Three studies of Lucian Freud, Francis Bacon – US$142.4 million**
4. No. 5, 1948, Jackson Pollock – US$140 million
5. **Woman III, Willem de Kooning – US$137.5 million**
6. Portrait of Adele Bloch-Bauer I, Gustav Klimt – US$135 million
7. **The Scream, Edvard Munch – US$119.9 million**
8. Flag, Jasper Johns – US$110 million
9. **Nude, Green Leaves and Bust, Pablo Picasso – US$106 million**
10. Anna's Light, Barnett Newman – US$105.7 million

1893

1954–1955

1968

1932

Maree man

This is the largest human art figure ever made. It was carved into the ground in Australia and measured 4.2 km long. It appeared in 1998, and could only be seen from the air. No-one knows who made it or why.

4.2 km

Micro art

Willard Wigan from the UK creates microscopic sculptures. They are so small that they can sit inside the eye of a needle.

Actual size

TUNE TIME

These artists really are the top of the pops! They've sold more songs and records than anyone else, had their songs played more times, had more number ones and had longer recording careers than any other acts on the planet.

Top selling artists (digital singles)

The best selling digital single ever is **I Gotta Feeling** by the Black Eyed Peas. Released in 2009, the song has been downloaded more than 8 million times.

Katy Perry	72m
Taylor Swift	66.5m
Rihanna	52m
Kanye West	32.5m
Lil Wayne	32m

Most No.1 Albums

Having sold more than 42 million copies since its release in 1982, **Thriller** by Michael Jackson is the best-selling album of all time.

10
Bruce Springsteen
Elvis Presley
Barbara Streisand

Most played tune

The Disney tune **It's a Small World** may be the most played tune in world. It's more than 50 years old and it is played continuously at all of the company's theme parks. It may have been played **more than 50 million times**.

During a 16-hour day, it's played 1,200 times.

Longest career

The record for the longest career as a recording artist belongs to Judy Robinson. She released her first record in **1926** and her last recording was made in **2003**.

77 years

Fastest selling

278,000

The American singer Taylor Swift holds the record for the fastest selling digital album in the US. In **2010, it was downloaded 278,000 times** in just one week.

MOST SUCCESSFUL RECORDING ARTISTS OF ALL TIME
(WORLDWIDE SALES – MILLIONS)

1. **The Beatles – 600**
2. **Elvis Presley – 500–600**
3. **Michael Jackson – 300–400**
4. **Madonna – 275–300**
5. **Elton John – 250–300**
6. **Led Zeppelin – 300–300**
7. **Pink Floyd – 200–250**
=8. **Mariah Carey – 175–200**
=8. **Celine Dione – 175–200**
9. **Whitney Houston– 170–200**
10. **AC/DC – 150–200**

Most records

In 1975, the British rock band Led Zeppelin became the first band to have six albums in the charts at the same time.

13
Jay Z

19
Beatles

Streaming music

Songs played on internet streaming services, such as Spotify, now account for **more than one-quarter** of the music industry's earnings.

Record piano players

In 2012, the record for the greatest number of musicians playing a piano was set when 103 people took it in turns to play part of Beethoven's Ode to Joy at a concert in Japan.

BEST SELLERS

Every year, billions of books are bought and read either in printed form or on e-readers and tablets. The people on these pages know what makes a good read. Meet the most successful, most prolific and biggest selling authors of all time!

Shakespeare Records

As well as being the world's best-selling author, William Shakespeare is believed to have invented, or introduced, more than **1,700 new words**.

His longest play, Hamlet, has 4,042 lines and 29,551 words. The character of Hamlet alone has 1,569 lines.

All of his works were recited over 110 hours in 1987 during the longest ever theatre performance.

Most filmed author

420 films and TV movies

Hamlet 79 movies

Romeo and Juliet 52 movies

Macbeth 36 movies

Largest Book

The largest book in the world is **This is the Prophet Mohamed**, published by the Mshahed International Group, Dubai. **It measures 5 m by 8.06 m, and weighs 1,500 kg.**

That's **taller than a giraffe** and weighs more than 20 adults, or **about the weight of a car**.

BEST SELLING AUTHORS OF ALL TIME (ESTIMATED SALES)

1. **William Shakespeare** 2–4.5 billion
2. **Agatha Christie** 2–4 billion
=3. **Barbara Cartland** 0.5–1 billion
=3. **Danielle Steel** 0.5–1 billion
5. **Harold Robbins** 800 million
=6. **Georges Simenon** 500–800 million
=6. **Charles Dickens** 500–800 million
8. **Sidney Sheldon** 400–600 million
9. **Enid Blyton** 350–600 million
10. **Robert Ludlum** 300–500 million

The Way to Happiness

by L. Ron Hubbard is the most translated book in the world. It can be read in 70 different languages, including Samoan and Uzbek.

Largest bookstore

The world's largest bookstore is Barnes & Noble in New York City, USA. It covers **14,330 sq m, the size of nearly 2.5 football pitches.**

... and has **20.71 km of shelves.**

Lauran Bosworth Paine
1916–2001 **850 books**

Kathleen Lindsay
1903–1973 **904 books**

Ryoki Inoue
1946– **1,086 books**

Edward Stratemeyer
1862–1930 **1,300 books**

Corin Tellado
1927–2009 **4,000 books**

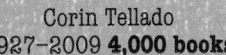

Most prolific writers

=100 books

GLOSSARY

‹••›

agility
To be able to move around, perform actions, and change the position and direction of the body easily.

album
A collection of songs or music recordings.

cells
The smallest parts of the body. There are many different types of cell, and they combine in different ways to form all the body's structures.

circulatory system
A collection of organs, tissues and cells – including the heart and blood vessels – which helps to transport blood, and the oxygen and nutrients it contains, around the body.

digestive system
A network of organs, tissues and cells that work together to take in food, extract its nutrients and expel any waste products.

digital single
A song or a piece of music that exists only as a digital file that can be downloaded.

dynamic apnea
A type of diving where people see how far they can go underwater just by holding their breath and not by using any special breathing apparatus.

endurance
The ability to withstand something, put up with something or do something difficult for a long period of time.

e-reader
An electronic device for storing and displaying electronic written content, such as a book or newspaper.

enzyme
A type of protein produced by the body which aids certain chemical reactions.

gross domestic product
The total value of the amount of goods and services produced by a country over the course of a year.

immune system
A collection of organs, tissues and cells that help to protect the body from infection and disease.

inflation
The process of things becoming more expensive over time.

life expectancy
The average age a person can expect to live to. It can vary from country to country, and from age to age. Before the era of modern medicine, people had a much lower life expectancy.

motor neurone
A type of long cell that runs through the spine and carries messages to the body's muscles in the form of tiny electrical signals.

nanometre
A tiny unit of measurement equal to just one billionth of a metre.

organ
A part of the body that carries out certain tasks or functions. The brain, heart and liver are all organs.

prolific
Producing a lot of work.

skeletal muscle
Muscles that are attached to the skeleton and give the body its shape. They can be consciously controlled and moved via messages from the brain.

stop-motion film
A type of film where models or objects are filmed, and then moved, one frame at a time. When shown at normal speed, this makes it look as if the objects are moving on their own.

streaming
Listening to or watching a digital file, such as a song or a film, over the internet in real time.

WEBSITES

MORE INFO:

http://science.nationalgeographic.com/science/health-and-human-body/human-body/
Get facts, photos, videos, games and more about the human body with National Geographic.

http://www.guinnessworldrecords.com
The website for all things record-breaking. It is packed with thousands of world records and facts.

http://www.bbc.co.uk/nature/humanplanetexplorer/
Discover incredible human stories from around the world with this BBC website.

MORE GRAPHICS:

www.visualinformation.info
A website that contains a whole host of infographic material on subjects as diverse as natural history, science, sport and computer games.

www.coolinfographics.com
A collection of infographics and data visualisations from other online resources, magazines and newspapers.

www.dailyinfographic.com
A comprehensive collection of infographics on an enormous range of topics that is updated every day!

INDEX

‹‑‑‑‑‑‑‑‑‑‑‑‑‑›

Acknowledgements

First published in 2015 by Wayland

Copyright © Wayland 2015

Wayland
338 Euston Road
London NW1 3BH

Wayland Australia
Level 17/207 Kent Street
Sydney NSW 2000

All rights reserved.

www.hachette.co.uk

Series editor: Julia Adams

Produced by Tall Tree Ltd
Editor: Jon Richards
Designer: Ed Simkins

Dewey classification: 301-dc23

ISBN: 9780750287494
ebook ISBN: 9780750287500

Printed in Malaysia
Wayland is a division of Hachette Children's Books, an Hachette UK company.

The website addresses (URLs) included in this book were valid at the time of going to press. However, because of the nature of the Internet, it is possible that some addresses may have changed, or sites may have changed or closed down, since publication. While the author and Publisher regret any inconvenience this may cause the readers, no responsibility for any such changes can be accepted by either the author or the Publisher.